baby steps

READ TALK PLAY

baby steps to reading

Carol McDougall and
Shanda LaRamee-Jones

NIMBUS
PUBLISHING
NIMBUS.CA

T0002208

How do babies learn to read?

Reading begins at birth, with your baby cuddled in your arms, listening to the sound of your voice. As your baby grows, they will start to reach for the book, point at things that interest them, and begin to turn the pages.

Your baby is listening to you and will begin to babble and imitate the sounds and words they hear. From birth, your baby is making baby steps to reading with every story you share. In time they will connect the joy of being cuddled and hearing your voice with a love of reading.

You are your baby's partner in this exciting journey, so make time to read together every day—it will become the best part of the day for you and your baby.

Let's Read

**Carol McDougall and
Shanda LaRamee-Jones**

baby steps

"I'm growing bigger every day.
Look what I can do!"

Look at Me Now!

text by
Carol McDougall and
Shanda LaRamee-Jones

Hold me close and read to me

Cuddled warm and tight

Your voice is like a lullaby

That soothes me day and night.

I am listening

Turn the page and show me

Pictures in a book

Polka dots and big red blocks

Let's take another look!

I am seeing

Polka dots...

So many books to play with

Spread out across the floor

Touch it, hold it, chew it!

That's how I explore.

I am reaching

Look at that, a big brown cow!

Can you see it too?

Tell me what a cow says

Does a cow say *moooooo*?

I am pointing

Turn the page and **peek-a-boo**!

A baby smiles at me

My turn now, *I'll* lift the flap

Now what can we see?

I am curious

Bedtime is our snuggle time

It makes me feel just right

Every night I pick a book

What will we read tonight?

I am choosing

I'm learning all about the world

Through every book we share

There's so much more to explore

Books take me **everywhere**!

I am ready
to read!

How do babies learn to talk?

From birth, your baby is listening to you. Babies need to hear words to learn words, so talk to them as you go about your day. Tell stories, read aloud, or recite a rhyme or two.

Rhymes let your baby hear the individual sounds in words. These sounds are the building blocks of your baby's early language. Chanting a familiar rhyme can also comfort your baby or entertain them when you're out and about.

The rhymes in *Let's Talk!* have been adapted from traditional nursery rhymes to show how you can take a favourite rhyme and make it your own. You can find the traditional rhymes that inspired *Let's Talk!* at the back of this book.

Let's Talk

Carol McDougall and
Shanda LaRamee-Jones

baby steps

Pat-a-cake, Pat-a-cake,

Baby's wide awake

You can say **PAT-A-CAKE**

THAT's what we'll make –

banana pancakes!

Down by the front door,

early in the morning

We are getting ready – ready to go

You can say **BYE BYE**,

we all wave bye bye,

Kiss kiss, bye bye, off we go!

This little baby went to market

This little baby ate a plum

You can say **PLUM**...

yum, yum, yum!

Baby ate a plum,

all the way home.

Rock-a-bye baby

Up we go...ZOOM

You can say up...**UP, UP, UP**

Over the moon!

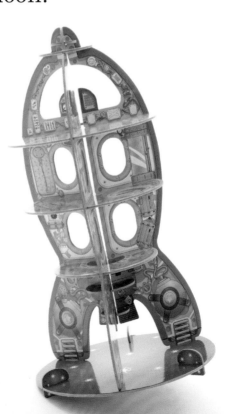

Rub a dub dub

   Splashing in the tub

You can say bubble....

   BUB, BUB, BUBBLE

Rub a dub dub!

Hush little baby

Time to count sheep

ONE TWO THREE FOUR

Sleep, baby, sleep.

Why is play important?

Play is how babies learn about the world. When you play with your baby, you are giving them love and attention and helping them develop fine motor skills. You and your baby can play together throughout the day—during bath time or a diaper change, or when you are out and about.

Follow your baby's cues. When your baby is ready for play, they will make eye contact, babble, or reach for you. When they are ready to rest, they will let you know by squirming or turning away.

What your baby loves best about play is spending time with you!

Let's Play

Carol McDougall and
Shanda LaRamee-Jones

baby steps

Baby, baby

> looking at me

Who do you see?

> Do you see me

> looking at you?

I LOVE looking at you!

Baby, baby

crawling to me

Two little hands

reaching for me

I'm reaching for you

I LOVE cuddling you!

Baby, baby

   strolling along

What's that you hear?

A chickadee song?

   Chick-a-dee-dee

   all day long

We LOVE strolling along!

Baby, baby

    peeking at me

Who can you see?

    Peek-a-boo you

    peek-a-boo me!

We LOVE peek-a-boo........SEE!

Baby, baby

turning away

What's that you say?

Had enough play?

Well...that's ok

Enough for today

Baby, baby

    quiet and calm

What's that I see?

Is that a yawn?

    Then I'll rock you to sleep

    with a lullaby song

Sweet dreams, my baby

    I love you!

Why are nursery rhymes important?

Babies love the rhythm and repetition in nursery rhymes. Rhymes break words into separate sounds. This helps your baby hear the individual parts of each word. When you chant a rhyme with your baby, you are helping them build their foundation of words and language.

Fun, bouncy rhymes will entertain your baby, while soft lullabies will calm and comfort them when it's time to go to sleep. Memorize a few favourite rhymes to entertain or soothe your baby wherever you go!

Traditional Rhymes to Share with Your Baby

Pat-a-Cake

Pat-a-cake, pat-a-cake, baker's man
Bake me a cake as fast as you can
Roll it, pat it, and mark it with a B
And put it in the oven for baby
    and me.

Down by the Station

Down by the station
Early in the morning
See the little pufferbellies
All in a row
See the stationmaster
Turn the little handle
Puff puff, toot toot
Off they go!

This Little Piggy

This little piggy went to market
This little piggy stayed home
This little piggy had roast beef
This little piggy had none
And this little piggy went "wee, wee,
    wee!" all the way home.

Rock-a-Bye, Baby

Rock-a-bye, baby, in the treetop
When the wind blows, the cradle
    will rock
When the bough breaks, the cradle
    will fall
And down will come baby, cradle
    and all.

Hush, Little Baby

Hush, little baby, don't say a word
Mama's gonna buy you a
    mockingbird
And if that mockingbird don't sing
Mama's gonna buy you a
    diamond ring
And if that diamond ring turns brass
Poppa's gonna buy you a
    looking glass
And if that looking glass gets broke
Poppa's gonna buy you a billy goat
And if that billy goat gets cross
Mama's gonna buy you a
    rocking horse
And if that rocking horse turns over
Mama's gonna buy you a dog
    named Rover
And if that dog named Rover
    won't bark
Poppa's gonna buy you a horse and
    a cart
And if that horse and cart fall down
You'll still be the sweetest little baby
    in town!

Rub-a-dub-dub

Rub-a-dub-dub
Three men in a tub
And who do you think they be?
The butcher, the baker,
The candlestick maker
And all of them going to sea.